The
Dryland Fish

An Anthology of Contemporary Iowa Poets

Edited by
Matthew MacLeod

1ˢᵗ WORLD
LIBRARY
Literary Society

•Austin •Fairfield •Delhi

The Dryland Fish

Edited by
Matthew MacLeod

© 1st World Library – Literary Society, 2003
809 South 2nd Street
Fairfield, IA 52556
www.1stworldlibrary.org
First Edition

LCCN: 2003116489

ISBN: 1 595409 96 3

Front cover image : "The Gate at Goemaat's Pasture- Section 22, Lick Creek Township, Van Buren Co., IA." Courtsey - John Preston
Back cover image : "Fencerow, Goemaat's Pasture-Section 22, Lick Creek Township, Van Buren Co., IA." Courtsey - John Preston

---

Readers interested in obtaining information on 1stWorld Library: •Publishing Services •Contributions •Book Conversion • Convert-On-Demand / Print-On-Demand contact www.1stworldlibrary.org

Iowa,
where a plane is a rising field
and a helicopter is a falling seed...

Acknowledgements

The editor would like to thank all of the poets who submitted their work for consideration to this anthology. My heart was warmed during the past Iowa winter and my mailbox was always full of entertaining poetry. This work is dedicated to all the writers who sent in poems for consideration -- those poets who are in these covers and those who are not. A tip of the hat to Charlie and Mazzy Knoles for inspiration with the anthology's title and to the anonymous Dryland Fisherman himself. Last, but not least, thanks to Betsy, Julie, Jennifer and Joan at Revelations Cafe for supporting local writers, musicians and artists and keeping the town of Fairfield, Iowa awake with fine coffee.

Steve Benson's "A Jury of Olives", "My Wife's Lovers", "Living in Obscurity" and "On A Hillside Facing West" are from his chapbook *A light In The Kitchen* (Blue Light Press, 2002). All are reprinted with permission of the author.

Diane Frank's "Planting Flowers In The Intuitive Garden" was first published in the anthology of contemporary Iowa Poets: *Voices on the Landscape* (Loess Hills Books, 1996). "Dancing at Old Threshers" is from *The Winter Life of Shooting Stars* (Blue Light Press, 1999), "Inseminating The Cows" is from *The All*

Night Yemenite Cafe (Dark River Press, 1993). All poems are reprinted with permission of the author.

Susan Klauber's "Iowa Land" is from *Face-off at Center Ice* (Blue Light Press, 1997) and is used with permission of the author.

Carole Lee Connet's "The Town Clock" is from *Searching For Entrance* (Half Angel Press, 2001) and was first published in *NYC Big Apple*.

Rustin Larson's "Melons" first appeared in *Cimarron Review* and reappeared in *Voices of the Landscape* (Loess Hills Books, 1996). "Both Halves Together" first appeared in *Panoply*. "Something Visceral" is taken from *Beyond 9-11*. "Robespierre Is Dead" first appeared in *The MacGuffin*. "To The Muse" first appeared in *The G.W. Review*. "The Electric Moon" originally appeared in *Loonfeather*. "Recovering" was first published in *Lyrical Iowa*. "Cedar River" first came to print in *The North Warren Town and Country News* and "The Des Moines Rising at Bentonsport" was first published in *Forty Days and Forty Nights* and is used with permission of the author.

Robin Lim's "Won't Need To Say A Word" was first published in the National Federation of States Poetry Society Prize Poem Anthology 2000 where it won 2nd place. "Stoop Berries" first appeared in *Bamboo Ridge, Hawaii Literary Magazine #89*. "Painting Carolyn's Bedroom in August" was first printed in *Midwifery Today 2002*. "Overcast" first appeared in an anthology, entitled *Short Fuse,* published by *Rattaphalax*.

Virginia McGuire's "Onion" and "Laundry" were

published in her first book of poems *Voices Under Water* (Blue Light Press, 1997). They are used with the author's permission.

Susie Niedermeyer's "Polishing the Quiet" first appeared in *The Iowa Sierran* and has been included with her permission.

Contents

Introduction

"The Dryland Fish...what on earth is that?" people ask. I'd always wondered so myself. Actually, until about a month ago I'd never heard of the thing. I had nearly finished sifting through the hundreds of poems I received for a contemporary anthology of Iowa poetry but was without a title. One night I was sitting in a booth at the 2nd Street Cafe, the only place for one to sit past 10pm on a weeknight in Fairfield, Iowa. A man walked in with whiskers and a pair of rubber boots that went up to his knees. He looked like he had been walking through the fields and left mud footprints across the tiled floor. I'm not one to apprehend a stranger, especially when a person is close to 6'3" like this man was, but I did keep an eye on him. He walked up to the counter where no one was and tapped once on the service bell. No one appeared. He looked slightly irritated. I could hear pots and pans sounding from the kitchen. Perhaps the sizzle of a radio drowned out the sound of the counter bell. *"Do you have any dryland fish?"* he hollered towards the swinging kitchen doors and then, before anyone could answer, stormed out the door, exposing a sliver of prairie sky.

I never saw the man again and soon forgot the details of his face but *Dryland Fish* swam about in my head for days. I didn't know what *Dryland Fish* meant but it would have to be the title for the anthology. The following week I learned that *Dryland Fish* is another name for "morels", the mushrooms which Iowans search the woods for, high and low, each spring. For two weeks in late April or early May nearly everyone collects morels which are these large, sponge-like mushrooms considered to be a mid-west delicacy. They sell them across local radio stations, on street corners from the open backs of run-down pick-up trucks and at local farmers markets. If you walk the county trails you'll see men trampling through the woods and prairie grasses carrying bags of them across their backs. I am told that they taste divine until they begin to go bad at which point they start to reek like rotten fish!

The word *morels* *is* dangerously close to the word *morals*. For most of the year, as I spent my time gathering poems for this anthology, I may have been collecting morals. Out of curiosity I went looking for a specimen of *dryland fish* one day on my own two feet but returned empty-handed with nothing more than the dirt on my shoes and a mild case of poison ivy. I missed the boom, bust and echo of the morel season but I did come across some superb poems. The writers in this book are all living or have lived in Iowa. Many are from *a speck on the map* called Fairfield which is also known as *a map on the speck*: some are teachers of the language, some are librarians, one is a world class bagpipe player and maker, another a famous radio personality, some are full-time writers, many are teachers of transcendental meditation, one is a mid-wife, another works on a Japanese fishing boat, some are currently unemployed, some are engaged and others fancy-free. And now from the fields of Iowa, without further ado, I introduce to you *The Dryland Fish.*

Matthew MacLeod
Summer 2003
Fairfield, Iowa

Writing a Poem on Company Time

- Tom Lemay

Writing a poem on company time
reminds me of advice given to me long ago
by the sage Vinnie Bruno, the Elder
encouraging me thusly: Every day steal a chicken.
As if this were the secret of life:
Every day steal a chicken!

Shackled to my cubicle,
bound to my computer and my telephone,
I'm at the mercy of the powers that control
my life, all of our lives with tediousness.

But still, to simply stop and give my attention to this
is a small act of rebellion; an insurrection of the spirit
that redeems my day and makes bright
this world of gray tones.
A little hunting and pecking on my word processor and I am
free, liberated, soaring
with the angels above the fruity plains.

And I'm getting paid to do it!

Like Gabriel with his trumpet
I have a message!

Every day steal a chicken!
Now let the walls come down.

Interstate Round

- Glenn Watt

I am driving down the Interstate. The music is turned up so loud inside, I can barely stand it. The hills are on fire. Every leaf of every tree is on fire. I unbutton my chest and let them pass through. They enter me like lovers, each one alive, penetrating and whole. We remain connected for awhile after they pass. Then I snap forward, like a long arm, to embrace the next. I am dancing down the Interstate. The music is turned up. I can barely stand it. My heart is on fire. Each leaf of every tree is dancing. Someone is driving. I am on fire. The music is whole. The lovers are dancing. Each leaf passes through me. My chest is unbuttoned. The hills are turned up. The music is dancing. The lovers are on fire. Each leaf is unbuttoned. The Interstate is dancing. Each leaf is whole. The hills are unbuttoned. The music is on fire. The dancers are dancing. The lovers pass through.

Interlude at Lamson's

- Glenn Watt

Mind like a spring pond
just released from winter's cold embrace,
calm and clear this morning,
a little lull before the rains,
green-backed turtles lazy, playful
in the still chilly shallows,
bumping up against one another
on a half-submerged limb
to bake in the sun,
nasal cheek of nuthatches
flirting hungrily among the trunks
of hickory and white oak,
the tall columns of the oaks
holding up the silence like a roof,
the silence notched and laced
like these snags arching
over the turtles' backs,
rough willow crotch at water's edge,
head high, the seat
where I sit, like anybody
happy for a moment to lounge
in the warmth and sunlight,
desires soughing like the wind
in the leafless branches overhead.

Inside The Grove
- Glenn Watt

The boughs grew close and thick.
Each twig-snap rang.

Forced to a creep, all our senses pitched,
we glassed the shadows for silhouettes
and shit-streaked bark.

Any other sign was lost beneath a sift of snow.

Once, we faltered, breaking through one end.
Had we, crippled by our eagerness,
stumbled blindly past them?

But doubt, like a doorway, only nudged us deeper in.

Who could have guessed
a   great horned?   would give them up
when it spooked like a gatekeeper overhead?

Tucked up under the boughs,
three jittery owls, the size of small crows,
in camouflage posture –

stretched tall and thin

pretending to be dead stubs on the limbs.

The long feathered ear tufts perched,
just as promised,
alertly on top their tawny heads.

And coupled with the rusty facial discs,
gave each a look –

our sudden presence as strange to them
as theirs was to us –

of permanent astonishment
in which two   unreadable? unanswerable?
yellow gold eyes glowed.

Giggling softly to ourselves, we watched them
as they watched us, shifting
from limb to limb, from look to look so long
they eventually calmed and settled back down,

lulled even into letting their large, feminine eyelids droop.

We took our time with them in the cold and fading light,
and grew a little giddy at their feet.
After all, we had come a long way to pay
obeisance to owls.

The Fool
- Glenn Watt

This evening,
I take my tea to the back step
and sit against the house.
My sitting rock beneath me –
like a large loaf of bread
fresh from the oven –
is still warm from the afternoon sun.
I look out at the garden
and at the afterglow of the sunset
and begin to re-build
the castle of love and joy
within me.
This time, it comes easily,
the spires and minarets soon reach
all the way to the heavens,
the foundation dug deep into the ground,
and I know my time has come.
And soon I get up
and begin to dance around the garden.
I hope no one is watching,
but I don't really care.
My arms are up,
the moon, almost full,
is shining through the neighbor's trees,

and our cat, white as the moon,
is catching bugs at my feet
as I turn, bow and spin
quietly as a fool
around and around among the flowers.

This One's For Me
- Glenn Watt

First cold snap of the season,
tomatoes wilting like hopes on the vine,
chiggers and ticks tucked, like naughty children,
safely back into their winter bins.

It's so easy to discount this landscape --

votive prairie turned to soybeans and corn,
conspicuous absence of the monumental, of something
we can get lost in.

In its stead, a hidden slip of wildness along Cedar Creek,
still green palms of the maples stained with sunlight,
enough warmth tossed about
to take the edge off a stiff northern breeze.

Here, bucking the chest-high grasses,
the snarl of currant and gooseberry and multiflora rose,
as always, the hesitation...

this not wanting to disturb the wood ducks
spiffed up like dandies in the dead branches
draping a solitary spit of sand,
to send the butterball turkeys squabbling

through the bamboo-like saplings
planted row upon row along the flood plain,
this not wanting to offend...

as if the earth could resent the intrusion.

A fence line I drive myself up against again and again --

nothing over there but an old frog pond
and a hillside of third growth timber,
nothing over there but a flock of goldfinches
delicately fingering the pale lips of willow and birch,
their nervous twitter momentarily lost
in the chatter of dying cottonwood leaves.

White-Throated Sparrows

- Glenn Watt

So we find say a patch of grass,
or the uprising fork of a dead trunk,
and we sit and watch and wait.
What are we looking for? What
do we expect to find?
A Philadelphia vireo flits by.
A hermit thrush, after preening itself, steps out
and thrashes for grubworms in the leaves.
The world is what it is.
It is a flock of white-throated sparrows,
the one we spooked off when we arrived, returning.
It doesn't hate us. It doesn't even care.
It scatters when we approach.

Eagle Days
- Glenn Watt

for Jack

In Iowa in the winter, it rains --
the road grows suddenly slick with it,
and we have to inch our way the last twelve miles,
pulling over onto the gravel twice
for Search and Rescue,
their electric red and blue flashing
against the wet gray dawn.

~

At Lock & Dam 19,
the biggest drop on the Mississippi,
the frigid water plunges thirty-eight feet,
stunning fish and churning the surface
a quarter-mile downstream.
Fiercely territorial in summer,
every winter the eagles grow comradely,
drift south in singles and small groups
from Canada, the Great Lakes
to congregate here, like a meeting of bishops,
the largest gathering in the lower 48,

and feed, as they have for hundreds of years.

~

Huddling in the rain shadow of the 136 bridge,
in the drizzle at the spillway overlook,
we pass binoculars, like steaming cups, between us.
All around, dark silhouettes loiter
like large incongruous leaves on the branches of trees,
like clear cut stumps on distant rim ice,
languidly sweep open water for dazed fish.
White head feathers bristling with weather;
relentless, ever-watchful yellow eyes,
the massive hooked beaks trunking out between them;
gripping talons marking them as raptors:
fish-eaters, carrion-eaters, graspers of prey.

~

In the small Midwestern walking mall,
downtown Keokuk, people flocked
from as far as North Carolina, California
graze the vendors, crowd the theater
for a live demonstration.
Still in adolescent plumage,
left eye socket vacant from a fledgling infection,
a two-year-old male perches on the leathered forearm
of a young blond Minnesota woman,
beak inches from her eyes,
and spreads his mottled bronze and white
six foot wings overhead.
A mature twenty-year-old flightless male
like a judge in regal wig and robes
educates us with his stubs.

Caught in a toe trap for coyotes,
he beat and beat at the ground with his wings
until all the slender finger bones were pulverized
to the wrists.

~

We buy a bag of fresh, fire-roasted,
lightly carameled popcorn from a thirty gallon tub
for the hour and a half drive home.
The temperature has tipped into the forties,
the road lost its glare,
and we travel quietly, my wife, my kids and I,
mostly in our own thoughts.

~

Sleepily topping a rise around midnight
on South Pass in the Wyoming Rockies
twenty five years ago, our blinding high beams
and howling fury suddenly bearing down upon him,
the eagle, feeding late on fresh road kill,
throws himself skyward, outstretched wings
completely blocking the view, chest muscles bulging,
the huge claws extended just clearing the windshield,
our startled faces whizzing by underneath.

*In commemoration of the bald eagle's
imminent release this spring from the
federal endangered species list, Jan '99*

A Jury of Olives

- Steve Benson

We struggled on bicycles into the country,
where they toppled like skeletons in the ditch,
ticking in the weeds -- spokes slicing sunlight.

We stepped between barbed wire, crossing a meadow
and smoothed a blanket over the bank of a creek.
Near the water hundreds of yellow butterflies
opened and closed their wings on the mud
like a town on tents.

Before unpacking the cold chicken and lemonade,
we sampled each other's tongue.

I wish I could say our tanned limbs tangled
as paired butterflies spiraled into the sun
like the twisting pillars of Love's Blue Temple.

But when we kissed all we shared was spit.
Buttons became equations beyond our intellect.

We shivered in the middle of all that heat.

The Rose never bloomed a rose behind our
eyelids. The earth never bucked beneath

our bare backs. The greasy chicken legs
and breasts slid down our silent throats.

The olives' tired red eyes accused us
from their tight glass house in the grass.

The lemonade soured in our wordless mouths.

Dust Devil
- *Steve Benson*

Passing a shallow ravine where rusty
trash was tossed, chewing timothy
arrows feathered with seeds,

I heard tiny clattering behind me.

Stopping and turning, I saw an animal
of air spinning toward me along a draw,
gathering bits of leaves, straw, twigs...

I stood there watching this spiraling power
stirring and mixing the world's ingredients.

Only a dust devil, but it made me feel
like a dust dweller. Like a whirling dervish,
a dance with nature we never finish, energy
turned itself visible by propelling pieces
of this planet into its clear pockets.

I loved this tuned-up engine of air
running without worrying about where.

Sliced by a wire fence near young corn,
it paused, as if bewildered or simply tired,

then, like a god slowly undressing on
a nameless little hump on a hill's belly,
it dropped all it held and disappeared.

Rabbit Algebra
- Steve Benson

To run is an impulse
quickly expressed by a rabbit
when school is out
and all the rabbit
chasing children
have chased each other away.
A rabbit jumps
from camouflaged complacency
into figure/ground relationships
that more times than not
do not end well.
Here comes a riding
lawn mower driven by a cigar
chewing custodian who bangs rocks
against windows and bricks.
He overlooks the rabbit
which the rabbit sees
or tries to believe
as it poses perfectly,
not even its eyes moving
or nose twitching, wind
combing cozy fur.
He looks like he thinks he's safe,
estimating threats

in a kind of rabbit equation:
safety is equal to distance
from danger divided by
speed of escape.
Carrying the bouncing custodian
the lawn mower dwindles
into green and blue,
drawing its roar with it,
diminishing to one dog
yelping on the horizon.
Silently the rabbit slips
between lilacs where
hollow dandelions
launch silky
parachutes.

Sandman Dates Tooth Fairy

- Steve Benson

They trust him to slip
into their dim rooms and sprinkle
crystallized dreams over lashes and lids.

Children debate if he should date
the Tooth Fairy saddled with her blue
bag of ticking rootless hollow milk teeth.

These two rendezvous at a sidewalk cafe
before dawn, and talk work while does
and fawns taste wet lawns.

The Tooth Fairy reaches under a wet
table and pets with a pickpocket's precision
the Sandman's dark leotards sewn with rhinestones.

The two collate kids' dreams drifting out of seaquence
Cute cars called Cindy or Sammy, with nothing
but fun under their propped bonnets, purr

down fired tunnels where fatherly
trees lift their bleached hairy roots,
then dance in circles around standing stones

woven with spirals and chevrons of migrating geese
During dutiful daylight the Sandman works
with busy city crews repairing

streets and playground equipment where warring
kids cavort, some missing a tooth and some
a little aggressive from lack of sleep.

The Tooth Fairy punches a clock at City Hall
recording licenses for marriages, births,
deaths, divorces, boats and cars.

The only evidence of their relationship is this:
Tooth Fairy brushes sand from her breasts,
Sandman flicks teeth from his sheets.

My Wife's Lovers

- Steve Benson

They must wonder what she wants with me
besides the usual chatter, the clatter
of Christmas lights and lawn mower.

Yes, I'm jealous of my wife's lovers,
but only slightly since they also offer
me pleasures -- sliding over my arms, back, hips.

It breaks her rhythm when I touch her. "Yes, yes,"
she sweetly lies at my heavy-handed tries
while her eyelids flutter.

Her legs stiffen and her perfect toes
squash pillows while her lovers press
deeper at the center of her pleasure.

They move quickly, cunningly over her slowly
provoked body, waiting calmly to recover
what my blunt fingers fumbled.

Humbled, I slip sheepishly out of bed, clutching
my balled clothes to my goose-pimply skin,
leaving her lovers tapping private

codes on her breasts' pink keys,
with answers to her tests
before she poses questions.

I close the door quietly, remembering
to latch it carefully so our children
and pets won't pounce on her pleasure.

Dressing quickly in the hall, I look down
at my own calloused hands and recall
lost hours we logged together.

Later, my wife comes out of our bedroom
swinging her two relaxed lovers at her sides.
She glides into the kitchen. Smiles at me.

Takes a clear glass from a cupboard.
Fills it with cold trembling
liquid and swallows it all.

Living In Obscurity

- Steve Benson

We hear the delicate drilling, the tentative tapping
of a woodpecker propelled by the pulsing sun
pressing down like a lover's thumb.

Elders of our trees were recently manhandled
by a bleeping bulldozer when the Mayor
of Obscurity built a playground.

Hedgehogs, snakes, rabbits, squirrels, birds and mice
lived where the bulldozer leveled a slim wilderness
loitering against our frail wooden fence.

Now all that wildness is buried or gone, except for a few
new trees touching pruned limbs like a thinned gathering
of survivors ringed around the flat body of the ground.

Wind passes revelations near our ears. It says
meadowlarks still trill to thousands
like us in fallow fields.

Wind touches what towers over
or cowers under every rock and iris,
rearranging every animal and human hair.

Wind says there is no street it hasn't
swept or polished pouring through
or slowly stirred by staying.

Something wild winks beyond our lot. Is it
light shaped like wings? Or wings
catching the day's last light?

Something free flickers between the rotting slats.

On A Hillside Facing West

- Steve Benson

Shivering beside a stone lamb
on a hillside facing west
I'm surrounded by stones
level with my head.
Crows stall in the wind.
Their shining bodies
winged and hollow-boned
vanish in the sun.
I walk above rows
of quiet white bones
dreaming in blackness
holding their breath
beneath light's hum.
I lean against a stone
standing balanced here
for thirty-six thousand dawns.
It rises from the earth
and touches the withered
limb of an elm marked
with a red X, fate's
illiterate signature.
A dark wall of clouds
approaches from the north
as shadows darken

my face and hands.
One crow still
hovers over me
while I walk under
an oak tree pitching
acorns at my father's stone.
I pick an acorn from the rusty grass,
flick its textured cap,
rub my thumb over
its smooth dark eye
that knows how to open
into a thousand limbs.

Milkweed Pods
- Connie Larson Miller

During World War II things were rationed.
Grandpa Johnson saved a big ball of tin foil
made of gum and cigarette wrappers in the cupboard.

Milkweed pods were hoarded for the silky
substance inside the pods,
and it was used to manufacture parachutes.

Dorothy worked as a parachute seamstress.
And when the war was over she and her fiancee
married, her wedding dress made from a parachute.

Sixty buoyant years later they came to worship
from Pennsylvania on a Sunday morning,
seeds of goodwill still afloat.

I recall this couple
how love spills so effortlessly.
Milkweed opening.

Albert
- Connie Larson Miller

He pulls out his hearing aid
during coffee hour at church.
"Too much clatter," he says,
places it in his overall breast pocket.
Says sometimes he hears things he shouldn't
like couples talking dirty.
Other times he hears the angels.

Said his mama didn't want him to marry.
I guess some of those girls weren't
too nice at Number Nine School, suppose?
My mother always thought people
took advantage of Albert.
They gave him room and board
wore his pencil down to a nub in payment.

But today Albert is feeling just grand,
even heard the angels.
As he has a sip of coffee
half cream and chews his dream
bar full of raisins and nutmeats.
Heaven's a little closer now.

Bones
- Nynke Doetjes

- Let that be left, which leaves itself
-- Shakespeare

I

Death does not follow on my heels like a haggard dog
but dances in my flesh: my own skeleton
waiting for my skin to peel like old wallpaper.
Decay is the beginning of an endless present.

I am a rattle-boned woman pillowed by fat,
a tissue-wrapped trinket, boxed so it won't make noise.
My heart, like the wildly pounding sea,
is a metronome measuring brevity.

I rest my head on my own skull at night
and sleep not an inch from my death
as a scorpion lives with its sting.

II

I am curious about Death.
I tried to peek at him as a Japanese girl of high birth

might have glanced at her future husband
from behind a painted screen.

It is a joke: The sun god steers a chariot,
the moon god has a boat.
Wind sails the clouds
and Death rides the dust mote.

Yet to Death the moon is paper,
stars no more than scattered salt --
I a moth with singed eyes blindly courting bulbs.

III

I am a burl in the scrim of the universe,
Death a pair of scissors, intending to cut holes.

IV

Death studies me as a gypsy studies tea leaves.
He whispers: 'Don't suffer through life;
wear it like a loose garment.
Take it off. Let it drop.'

This means he wants my lips.

V

When I die I will shout at my heart:
'Lonely bird, fly up from your tree of bones!'
I will shout at Death:

'Have me! It will be like eating a cracker.'

VI

A coven of vultures will pick my remains
clean as silver needles.
My ashes will be pinned on some lake's chest,
fleeting medals of glory.
The wind, that flagellant who out of spite
keeps a whip next to his bed, will take the rest.

VII

The sun watches with a dry fish eye.

The sun is a riddle; it taunts the mind,
then disappears untimely -- its own elusive answer.

My bones whisper: 'You can only die
if you measure the world by day and night.
Look past the sun for freedom from death.
Ponder the rain.'

Dust

- Nynke Doetjes

Music is composed of notes, the body
of dust motes. Arrangement determines
color, size, shape. Open the shades.
See: dust motes twirl in ball gowns

of light, a floating suspension in each
movement as though they existed in alternate
ambit. String Theory speaks of eleven
dimensions: length, width, depth, time --

seven others undefined, coordinates
that serve to locate matter even if
it is rolled up like a sheet of paper.
This is the poetry of physics, poetry

of that common constituent which,
in the end, we must all kiss: dust.

Praying Mantis

- Nynke Doetjes

A praying mantis lifts two spindly arms
atop a viburnum at night. I stop to watch

the calm black space inside her eye that,
though small, contains a piece of sky.

She and I stare at each other. Her back
gleams lavender. Above, a street lamp

thinks it is the sun and showily pours
cold light down so we might think the same.

I watch the mantis -- watch her tendrils drift,
the jagged edges of her wrists, legs

in full repose but well-prepared to shift.
There is a tremble in her, not a motion

but the possibility of the beginning of a leap.
My nails press moons into my palm,

hands are fists. My buttoned coat strains
to keep a wild crow captive in my chest

that flaps mad wings, scans time in heartbeats --
fast -- against my ribs. I am so opposite.

I want to startle, stun, breathe her away,
hear the snap of sprig-like legs -- see her leap.

I cannot bear the stare we have exchanged.
She dropped the sky into my eye to keep.

The Rape

- Nynke Doetjes

I

Strewn on the beach: shells packed with sand,
mouths gagged with the stoic substance that marks
the passing of time -- inhabitants gone, claimed
by the tide, consumed by fish, shattered on rock.

The sea's lips are its fingertips; they speak
in imperative moans. Who can deny such orders?
Long ago, the occupants of these shells,
dressed well, were told to take off their clothes.

If they dared refuse, fingers of water pried
their entrances in a turbulence of waves,
weed and sand. The sea -- horny, wild,
indecent -- herded them in a lascivious chase.

Who hears the voice of the meek? It is certain:
the shell was not given a chance to speak.

II

Embracing rock, the sea's arms turn
flirtatious like frilly Elizabethan cuffs
and squash small things in indifferent love.
The hem of the sea's shirt comes loose on the shore;

its fingers reach everywhere, shaking
crustaceans from their homes, coins from purses.
The sand smoothed, one shell, once loose in the waves,
is caught in the hand of a child. The child washes

it clean, uses it perhaps to decorate
a sandcastle. When the child cautiously
presses the worn casing to its ear,
the shell begins to whisper. The child's father

explains: inside you hear the sea's roar.
How can a child understand such a cruel story?

First Memory
- Nynke Doetjes

Sunlight tumbles into the crystal ashtray
placed in the center of my parents' table,
from there flings across the wall, rainbow
of yellow blue purple red specks

darting with such blissful splendor
my heart stumbles in my chest, wishing
to dart along, then pushes, hot sun,
inside a dress I am convinced will rip,

not resilient enough to stretch -- pushes high
inside my frame until my head shoots
from the top of my neck, cork from a bottle.
Terrified, I flick inside out, leaping

ceiling, wall, floor in sacred play:
spider of light trying to get away.

Soldier's Daughter, 1949

- Nynke Doetjes

In the stable: a ten year old, cold fists
clutching a milk pail. Her father's words spill

to the ground around her feet. Shadows between cows
obscure this winter evening's secrets.

Before he came in she'd hunched in the farthest
recess of the barn, on her haunches, peed,

a warm small stream; it trickled, murmuringly,
between the planks of the floor. She'd hurried

her skirt in place at the echo of his footstep.
Now moon falls through the roof; she knows

how to catch its whiteness in her lap.
Her sturdy hands have begun to do the work of milking.

She cannot read his face. As he speaks, the nails
that stick out from the wood siding, crusted with rust,

seem necks without heads. She remembers his arm
wielding the old ax, now stuck in a wood block --

quick, sure stroke like the wing of a hawk;
it tore sky which stayed whole, wood which chipped

and bled sawdust. Tepid milk blood on her fingers,
moon blood on her father's cheek, hot nor cold.

The rattling of chains, the bark of a dog,
the soft shuffling shifts of the flanks of the cows

mix with words her mother forbids at the dinner table
in the confines of a proper house. There is a strip

of night dividing him and her but not an inch
of light between her and these stories.

She works the udder, sitting on hay. Until he leaves,
she will be thinking of something to say.

Mulberry Tree
- Elisa Fritsch

The skinny, lanky branches of the
mulberry tree
crowd around me
as I hunch, bend, and leap
to capture the nubs of berries.
The leafy taste of a black mulberry
waters my tongue.
Up into the tree I reach
quickly, greedily,
aching to fill, to replace
the dissolving berries in my mouth.
The soft, spurting collapse
of black flesh
under my teeth
and the tantalizing movement
of the branches
tell me
the tree enjoys
my caresses.

I reach under the mane of the tree
groping for the succulent berries.
Ouch! A mosquito
stings

the thin flesh of my elbow
but it is no match for the sweet pleasure
of the sour, mulberry taste.
The granular seeds, so small in the berry,
lie on my crooked teeth,
pulverized like sawdust.

My tongue
races
over each
cream colored tooth
wiping the purple extract
of mulberry juice.
Another mosquito quivers to the left,
but the wind sways the brown branches
and I step deeper,
closer, into the tall, spiky grass
under the arbor of the tree.

Surrounded by branches,
red and ripe berries,
I pause,
allowing the tree's anticipation
to last
until I thrust my hand
up the leg of one branch
and feast my fingers
on the hanging, black drops.
The blood of the tree
stains my shirt
and my lips grow tender
from exercise.
Soon, I stretch and wade out from my arbor.
The tree stands still.

Reaching out, I touch
the sandpaper bark
and mutter
excuses for love.
Sated, the tree collapses
its outstretched branches.
The birds flutter back
to their pockets,
and the tree
gives itself over
to the lesser pleasures
of the birds.

Ice Fishing In Iowa
- Tim Britton

Here the land swells slowly
keeping its head down
round shoulders are what you see
Like chest hair peeking from an open shirt
the trees speak quietly of the black earth
their toes secretly enjoy
keeping to the low places
where water stands and looks
running only under the surface
The wind moves effortlessly
no mountains to hold the gaze of the clouds

In winter
cold eventually comes
river and pond hold their gaze instead and
watch as wind rises and falls
Ice spreads and thickens
a window on waterweed, bass and bluegill
Oak leaves shiver
rattling amongst themselves
hollow reminiscence of acorns once known
The sun's cold stare from such a distance
reminds of its closer friends
more centrally located on the
fat belly of the earth

Dog
- Tim Britton

they know
that there's nothing to do
but lay there
yet the tail
thump thumps
on the floor
when our eyes meet

Tailspin
- Tim Britton

I feel like a baby
just learning to walk
being present
in this moment
dropping the talk
is both the only thing I can do
and the only thing I can't do
sometimes I hear
a thousand flies
buzzing around my ears
but it's really only one
let's face it
you and I
are really only one
and this music I'm playing
isn't it the same music
you've always danced to?
let's stop hiding behind these masks
of differences
or at least enjoy the show
for what it is
it is
isn't it?
who cares
dance with me

Inside me
- Tim Britton

is a wide open space
a high ceilinged cavern
lit up with citrus suns and galaxies
of iridescent reds and blues
where fairies live their hidden lives
and birds excitedly anticipate the dawn
before even the air turns blue

the space where fear
makes the alchemical change
into golden light
where creamsicle fountains
radiate with the joy of self knowing
a symphony of pearly notes
drips from the ceiling
into awaiting pools of color
where the floating leaves of last year's cognitions
when upturned by gentle fingers
reveal mantras
ready to transform
clay into song

a place where monks
bathe in silent joy

where flower devas
are not afraid
to come to you in person
to hand you their scented gifts
with a smile and a curtsy

The Old Iowa Garden

- Virginia McGuire

She combed a quarter-acre of dirt
with her fingers, sorrowing over the worms
the shovel had sliced.
It was all mapped out.
Flowers by the back door.
Herbs to the right of the path.
The furrows circled out
from the Saint Francis statue
as if he was a pebble.

Her bean teepee was a hasty leaning
masterpiece of sticks and string.
I helped her poke a dried bean
into the dark up to my first knuckle.
In a few weeks we introduced
sticky bean stalks to each string.
When they had climbed to the top
I sat inside on the weedy dirt
and saw glints of orange nasturtium
through the beans and the leaves.

It's best to water at night or in the morning before heat.
She did it in her nightie,
blinking, yawning, waving to the neighbors,

yelling at the dog to get out of the lettuce.
She'd press her thumb over the hose nozzle,
aim the fan of water clear over the kale
to the raspberry bushes that never yielded.
When the garden was dripping
and you could hear the roots starting to sip,
she'd take the heavy old metal can
and make house calls to the marigolds.
They stink but they're so pretty
and we planted them by the lilacs.

One year she climbed all the trees
along the back fence
and ripped out the poison ivy with her hands
because she was so mad at it choking our trees.
She itched for two months.
We had to stoop all afternoon sometimes
picking up the black walnuts
so the neighbor boy could mow.

Now she's moved across oceans
like we all do in this family,
leaving houses and pets
lovers and even children.
Her Hawaii garden has papayas
arugula, and six-inch centipedes
that send her to the hospital.

But the Iowa garden refuses to die.
In the house, the sills and the baseboards
are dusty. The doors squeak.
The dog lies with his head on his paws,
and the air in her bedroom is stale.
Out back I find the lettuce

gone to seed but thriving.
The raspberries need thinning
but they're alive and still fruitless.
I pinch off a few mystery leaves
and smell my mother's pasta sauce on my fingers.
Sage and basil and oregano grow wild
while she cooks with fresh coconut milk
and white ginger, half way across the world.

Full Time
- *Virginia McGuire*

Waking up in the dark to someone
who is this man?
shaking my shoulder
honey you have to work today
honey you have to get up
I refuse to believe it is morning
I refuse to believe this is civilized
life that requires the pulling of limbs
from cramped and warm rest to stand up
somehow and get to the sink?
oh yes to brush my teeth
and in this state I must find some reserve of life
force sufficient to get me twenty miles
into the suburbs to a desk
in torturous shoes and stained blouse
to stay upright like a stuffed scarecrow
all the day long until an invisible gate lifts
and the rats run back to their holes for
such a short night then tomorrow
god I can't think of tomorrow
I will be up and working and waiting for the
paycheck which means this is temporary
always saving so this will be temporary
this being ruled by invisible gates

until I find someone to pay for my real work
my writing
my writing is a dream I come back to before sleep
thinking after the deadline I will have time
after the product ships I will have energy
I will write I will do my time I will save my pennies
meanwhile writing furtive poems in the office
hiding the window behind others on the screen
racing to retrieve my real work from
networked printers I will write
I will not be a rat forever I believe this in order
to get out of bed.

Morning Commute to Manhattan

- Virginia McGuire

something cold spreading through
the train people
saying the smoke
   the smoke
could they mean those smokestacks
on the shore

man with phone
feeds us news through
a filter
we long for the prairie
   the corn
and the sky

the skyline wears smoke
like a mink
(Eric Gill waiting
at the club)
but
Pentagon
   Pentagon
Pentagon
fills the train
the station

the station is crazy
a voice strangely normal
calling Trenton Express
    boarding
I'm boarding
leaving the tunnel
we all breathe
one tower

one tower
our hearts beat one tower
    behind trees
and then

Onion
- *Virginia McGuire*

Peel off tight shoes, pale stockings,
oh breathing shins and thighs.
Buzz zipper off
rustle rayon wrinkles on the ground.
Blouse buttons--pop!
Tear silk collar
reclaim my neck
own myself.
Tug at elastics
tear out hair.
Who cares?

Free of ribbons and combs;
shake loose.
Stoop to gather heavy stones
Chinese farmer's wife.
Fingernails claw earth
perfect manicure broken, dirty.
Stand erect, pull arm back
let fly palm-sized boulder
egg shell shatter sound
a spiderweb in your windshield.

More stones, more weight.

Put some shoulder into it.
Throw them harder.
Dent hood, scratch paint
kick aside heaped clothes
loathed cocoon
looking for another rock.

Advance on cowering car.
Creep up on it.
Bludgeon your red Honda dream.
Bash in doors,
fragment windows.
Shards escape the melée.
Run away, panting,
still clutching weapon.
Leave feminine husk of rayon onion skins
in a pile like a signature
from the naked, bloodied vandal
who can't even hear herself
laughing.

Laundry
- Virginia McGuire

Our socks, two of mismatched
hundreds intertwined in the dryer,
but you never knew my last name.

My sister's red crinoline
is so bright it burns
my fingers as I hang it up.

When my dark load goes in
I sit on the dryer and it hums
beneath me like the mumbling of stars.

Iowa Land
- Susan Klauber

I

Tired land,
dried crumbles of corn,
beans scrunched in darkness.
The goddess is asleep, under a spell.

II

Buck and Irene
are names you find stamped on the wrought iron mailbox
shaped like an antique harvester,
a lone sentinel posted
quarter mile down the dirt road from the pink
hogs named Ethyl and Lou.

The church spire is a long way off,
too far to see over the pig huts and scrapers of corn,
mud sucking the fence posts into yesterday.
But you can hear the steeple chiming,
echoes running through the slop of rubber boots,
bull frogs' horns,
cricket hymns to Palm Sunday.

The screen door rattles shut.

III

American Red Cross first aid class Wapello County:
"The biggest threat to safety here are the trucks
transporting chemicals on the highways.
One drop of pesticide THIMET-COUNTER on your skin,
and you die.
One quart in the Des Moines River
and everything
from Ottumwa to the Mississippi
dies."

IV

Buck leans over the ceremonial hole
in the northeast corner of his land,
watching the Pundit chanting
foreign sounds like hymns to ancient memories
hidden inside the earth.
Or maybe it's the lost ages of Sac and Fox
trembling over the plains,
buffalo carcasses scoured from the trenches
left by cavalrymen on their way home from war.

A pink picture of geometric lines
converges into a lotus
empowered with the rule of Mother Earth,
Shri Yantra lowered into the northeast corner of their land.
A gift of invocation.
Return this land to Mother.

May we once again be servants
with Her lush harvest upon our brow.

V

"In Iowa cancer is rising.
Hard to imagine in the midwest!
Maybe it's the chemicals in the fields."
His graying ponytail turns away,
No one knows
buried by calloused hands
in the northeast corner
of the next chapter of the land.

3 Haiku

- Ila Zeeb

I

Crisp sound of bite
Breaking stretched skin
Of red apple.

II

Little dark birds
On electric line
Like notes of music.

III

Strong arms of traintracks
Reaching into the distance.
For whom?

Walking
- Michelle Demers

One foot in front of the other
a rhythm of clear light
and air that slides down my throat
like a mint, one foot in front
of the other, then a train lumbers by,
its huge weight in my chest
as it creaks and squeals over rails
one foot in front of the other,
tempo through my head, movement
driving me forward, a need for integration,
sailing into clouds, facing the
autumn winds, no silence now,
the noise of the world fizzes
into my consciousness, part
of the everlasting balance
like darkness and daytime, one foot
in front of the other, clears
the mystical spaces between
my cells, opens the secret
floodgates, the reverberations
that shake their way up my spine
and I know in this instant
that in one more step
I will lift off this earth.

Heart of Lightness
- Michelle Demers

On the surface
it looks like white bread America.
Town squares with gazebos,
Casey's General Stores,
18-wheelers on Route 1 rolling through small towns,
doughnut shops on street corners,
trucks full of squealing hogs,
video stores,
Wal-Mart,
McDonalds.

Then there's the sky.
It opens out
wide,
expansive.
You can breathe it in
and feel it fill you completely.

It comes in colors of sensations and emotions.
Pink and purple in the morning
Orange before a thunderstorm
Cornflower and violet on a summer day
Crystal blue in January
Slate in November

Crimson, royal, golden, green, and brilliant at sunset.

At night it is blacker than black,
intimate, deep, affectionate.
Expanding the darkness
into a heart of lightness.

The land opens out on all sides,
sometimes rolling
mostly flat,
offering itself for bounty,
the strength that is the earth.

From the tops of the tallest silos
you can see hog farms,
cornfields,
movie houses,
white picket fences,
drugstores with neon signs,
black squirrels,
oak trees.

The land takes it all in.
Sun scorching,
rains thundering and cleansing,
snow flying horizontally and purifying the blood,
wind blowing so fiercely you fight to remain standing.

In the center
where the land and sky mingle
is a mass of energy and non-energy
through which the whole world flows.
It attaches itself to your navel,
and leads out to the sky,

carrying the lightning back
on wild horses
across the wind-blown prairies,
home to the heart of lightness.

Melons

- Rustin Larson

You bought one, perfectly ripe,
but within days
little holes appeared
and it began to shrink from inside
like a consumptive.
Time after time we'd buy the sweet smelling globes
and they'd rot.
You said we had bad luck with melons.
I said we were cursed.

and so it was we wandered the earth dreaming
of the perfect incorruptible melon.
We would walk by a woman
and think of melons. We would walk by a man
with large knees and think of melons.
Even when we were spending money on clothes
we would think we were dealing out melon leaves,
thick and prickly, always leaving
a trace on our hands. Our shoes became
melon rinds, and our fingers, slivers of ripe
yellow melon. So when was it we stopped
thinking of these things? I think it was
the day in the supermarket when
you said to me, "Rus, I can't live

like this anymore!" and walked off,
leaving me to contemplate the absence of melons
and their traces, their juices and their mold.
"Why should I live like this either? I thought,
and sat down on a crate, and weighed
my big round head in my hands.

Both Halves Together

- *Rustin Larson*

Like the man who says, "It's my invention,
It came to me while I was on the john!"
I know exactly what to do with my life:

One half will repair the spines of dwarves,
So they will stand corrected; the other half
Will get to know our feathered friends better

Like a bitter colony of lice, will sit
In golden kinship as autumn smoke rises
From the leaves, will chew on a piece of

Celery and feel how good its stringy wateriness
Tastes in the open air. Both halves together
Will wish they had gotten into real estate

Early on, but mostly they will admire
Those who spent their lives serving humanity,
Those who rescued children from the jaws of mice,

Those who poisoned the silver-skinned men
From Pluto with orange juice, those who are
Tucked away in the ground with a few
Roses on top of them, and a few sweet words
Cut into the sadness.

Tell Me About the Wasp Again

- Rustin Larson

for Jacob Godwin-Jones

The brown wasp clinging to the porch screen?
He was awakened, fooled by warm weather.
Today, February blossoms: the wasp
looks at you and me who smash flowers
on the porch steps with a round stone.
Perhaps he wonders what we will do with all
the green nectar, or worries we will exhaust
the yard of white flowers he has some claim to.
So, maybe we are not being fair; maybe
we cannot reassure him that before long we will tire of it.
He is staring at you,
Jacob. You could squash him with a blow
of your tennis shoe. You could blow on
the screen and he would fly away.
Maybe he would jab one of us with his stinger –
the fine brown barb with a sack of poison that throbs heart-

like when its shaft is stabbed in flesh – but who says
we can't inhabit the same triangle of time unharmed?

We will not tap the screen
where the wasp suns himself. We will watch

as he builds his house from mud; the same mud
we were, Jacob, before these bodies
were spun, and our souls poured into them.

Something Visceral

- Rustin Larson

In this amber cubical on earth,
on a Thursday evening as it rains,
in a library near the books that deal

with the Mafia and finance,
as the trade centers lie in smoke and ruin,
I in Iowa with a few voices

and answers speaking to nothing
immediately near: the seeds the squirrels hoard,
the grasses still green, the apples

luxuriant again following a foul year.
Can we believe it all to end too soon?
We who feel, who can't let go of the body,

so it becomes the only song we sing,
though the rapture extends its great fiery arms,
though it extends its engulfing sleeves,

and the Lord smiles, and everything these
Jehovah's witnesses painted on their pamphlets
comes true, still

we the singers, the true sinners and lovers
of earth, remain coaxing a tyrant death
to sleep with our silent sibilance,

our thoughts, our rhythms and shaking,
though our teeth become castanets
and our intestines the strings

of hideous guitars,
we sing, we sing, and we
will not let go.

Robespierre Is Dead

- Rustin Larson

We spent the day at the National Zoo
Weaving our way past the monkey house
To where the elephant

Bathed: he tossed a truck tire
In the air like a toy.
I sipped my snow cone too far

Back and my white shirt
Drowned in purple and maybe
A splash of elephant snot

From Jumbo who was then
Spraying his audience. I was
Fat as hell and imagining

A world without mirrors as I
Tucked it under my belt
And flung on a spare

Polo shirt from my gym bag
And waddled to the penguins
Who could not grin but seemed

To be grinning anyway.
In the reptile house you couldn't

Breathe, so I dragged you out

Choking into the sun, your hand
Strangling my left love handle
And I thought everyone was worried

And confused, though on further
Reflection, I realized no one
Was watching us at all.

With a screech nearby
An orange monkey mounted
His wife and after three

Thrusts jumped to his perch
And fell asleep on a lump
Of his own excrement. Just about

That time, the hotdog stand opened,
So I decided to get a 7-Up to soothe
Your sick stomach. As I was waiting

I noticed a young man with dirty
Black hair thrown over his eyes,
Carving (with a sharpened spoon handle)

The phrase "Robespierre is dead" into
A turnstile. "Probably," you said,
"He killed him." As I looked back at the young man,

He was eating a snow cone near
The prairie dog mound.
How he smiled and crunched the ice

With his sharp purple teeth!

To The Muse
- Rustin Larson

When I think about the holy occupations
I carpe diem myself into submission.
The wall is myself and my ear
Hears the empty spaces that have
Made up this planet. I feel cured
In short. Knowing the right way to face
The wind, I walk into it, it doesn't
Bother me. There are certain terms
We have settled on—it knows it's
The same wind as Jamestown or
Plymouth. I have had my feasts there
And I continue to take them with
Me in this brown paper bag.
Instead of contradictions
It contains the resolutions in its
Emptiness. A violent emptiness is
The wind, and it can pick up whole
Houses, if it wants, piling them like
Crumpled egg shells in an open field.
The light falls upon all things. I have
My memory of you—quiet as a
Picture frame among all these broken houses.

The Electric Moon

- Rustin Larson

Drumming canyons of tall black air,
Drinking somnambulists,
The Greyhound rumbles, stops and so on
Through farmtowns' milky lights.

In Albia, the electric moon flashes
Pilsner ad: meteorites leaning
Into luminous pastel blue, bleeding
Threads of flame, white ice strobing
Through yellow shot glasses, the tavern

Door slapping under neon buzzing celestial.
One tired angel boards.
Toward daylight and Mt. Pleasant
Weather gears down into drizzle,

Snaking ice water through greening hills.
The angel sleeps, wings smoothed under her
Brown wool coat, head tilted toward
The window, the swimming
Phonographic grooves, stubbled fields.

Recovering
- Rustin Larson

Bonds of booze latched behind beveled wood
and glass. All day, the window: the bare
ground hard as iron; the woods, still
stone crosses. Strangely sentient, the un-
plugged telephone near the sleeping cat;
daughter drags in the latest cold from school,
mittening a paper collage of winter stars.
All night crystals dune at our door.

Morning, I get up from writing near the window
(the Christmas cactus flames) walk across
cold maple, slip on wool-lined boots and open
biting December. Warmth from the house vapors
into God-rutted cornfields: ivory Sahara.
I trot pushing daughter on her sled, icing
a run. I backfall into a drift, drunken with cold.

Cedar River

- Rustin Larson

As I walked to my room one night with all this longing and
love running through me like two unmixable rivers, I thought
of how hawk feathers sometimes rain from the branches that
hang over the Cedar River. And they spin down instantly
with no speed or smell and lip the water with clean light
affection and then glide like barges, sideways, bobbing to the
dimples and snarls in the brown season fostering current.

And when all objects have floated to the dam, I wait for the
sound the river has to bring me. It comes curling like a
golden wave—it happens to be the sound that hollowed the
mudbanks and exposed all the roots so they stream out of the
river wall like so many tangled thoughts or incommunicable
wires ripped from their cabled divisions. It is a curling sound
that comes, like the bending of branches, and those flutes
that are constructed for such an intangible length of time
offer their fluttering from the neck of trees—where one limb
becomes the next and then strikes the clouds with its own
lightning bolt.

Faulkner

- Rustin Larson

I wish I could show you the source of my amusement but I can't it was delivered in an ice box three hundred million years ago and it has been there since anticipating time or the mind that will discover time on the shores of some mossy simultaneously existing/non-existing primordial earth It sits there silent and square totally emotionless to the tiny grubs and centipedes that crawl over its smooth porcelain skin Totally inert but inside it is something that will outlast the shores and water even the sun and myriad furry life forms that will bump and crawl their way to the edge of their individual eternities It is there denting the sand silent unmoved not feeling hunger because hunger isn't yet thought of nothing there to think it not happy because happiness is still unboiled stagnant and cold as unreal as the possessions and human bodies that will someday give it birth.

The Des Moines Rising at Bentonsport

- Rustin Larson

River, quarter mile wide here, brown
as motor oil. Currents swirl an Amoco cup,
suck it down (fifty-three miles up
from the Miss) near a clinically dead town.

Foam dots the ripples like globs of spit
below the maples. Cottonwoods skirt the bank
as if calling the other side for thanks
or help. And orange in the leaves, orioles perhaps; it's

a difficult song, full of the confluence
of failure and rotten luck and grace
like undertow shadowed by the crusted iron

crisscross of a bridge. And brown moths dance
on the childish weeds of the bank, a face
on each wing, and water inches in like prairie fire.

A Love Story

- Meg Fitz-Randolph

for Tim

Twice I came to your new city in the first days of desire,
drove the snowy roads, overwrought, in my jumbled way
and lost my bearings, the sound directions you had given
where to meet, transmogrified by nerves. Looking back
I see the crisscrossed paths our lives became, a love story
full of misdirection and tenderness, all we meant to merge.

At Penn Station, to rendezvous at four, so sure of my way,
having waited all week, treading my life, no directions given,
you in the central waiting room, hours go by, but we're back
to back, you only inches from me, a rich girl in another story
waiting underneath a clock. From this dream, at last, I emerge
to your face (I'll always see it), amusement crossed with desire.

Then once again, coming to your new place, it's now a given,
you and me, dusk rolling in, streetlight shadows at my back.
I'm racing to your brand new building, 51st and 6th, 8th story,
wanting to fling myself on you, our bed of winter flowers,
merge this heat with your heat, not seeing clearly anything but
desire, these beams and planks erected, the correct address, a
stairway.

I need only to mount this stairway to the stars, then I'm back with you. Up and up, the street getting smaller, I pause in my story to see you climbing after me, softly calling my name, we could merge here, high above the main entrance with its pedestrian desires. We could claim our life, far from the everyday. It is still our way to look at stars together, to strew and misconstrue all we're given

Which has been larger that anything I could dream up as my story. Until now we find ourselves in this forest of moonlight, submerged under some spell we're at a loss to decipher, every nugget of desire granted us, the fairy daughter, castles of success, chosen pathways brightly lit, seem buried now. In a simpler time I'd ask to be forgiven the careless travesties, thanklessness, to bring our treasures back.

You'd lead me to our shelter in the woods, where the stars merge with valor, no one ever lost again. But in the real world I desire there remains a vigilance of doubt, odd crumbs along the way. Your goodness is a shelter blooming over us, no one ever gives or gets out of emptiness. What's worn away by time grows back. How we navigate these twists and turns also turns into our story.

The Gleaning

- Meg Fitz-Randolph

My little window at the Mississippi Abby
looks out across scruffed grass,
fields of tasseled corn, thistle and thorn,
greens and gold coming on autumn,
warmer air rising off
the leafy tops.

This wide valley, up from the legendary river
I can't see just yet, but is surely there
just the way the sister said
pointing over my shoulder to where
a thin feather of smoke plumed off that train
coming along just now, this side, our side,
of the river.

But I who only half-way saw (which means
not at all -- no, not yet) nod "*yes, yes*" and
"*I see, I see*" seconds, no minutes, before I did
see, the white veil hanging softly
in the air between us.

Not until I was alone again,
taking in the view for myself
from my own room, that I saw the brown thread

of water dimly moving, all but invisible.
That great border dividing
the vast from the vast.

2.

Here at my writing table rests a Madonna and child, the kind
    tourists
buy in Italy, triplet panels of Florentine blue flecked with
    stars

    where Rafaello's Mary harbors baby Jesus, her gaze
both inward and outward. The masters understood, it seems,
    what the world now

    hardly notices, that a life grows inside its own well

before turning, if it turns at all, to its metaphor of fields,

city and work. Her field of vision is both intimate and far
beyond what I fathom

    from the arched windows of her balsam house.

In Florence once, before the awful floods, before I learned to
see myself as anything

    but a dark well overhung with a frenzy of stars …

I saw this painting of Mary hanging with a hundred other
    Marys, where each

    gazed passively from her own arched window

in the worn and filtered light of the Ufizzi.

Now to have her here again, overlooking the abbey's last
    harvest,
awaiting the guests who've come like myself, worn and in
    need,

is not surprising except...except here she is with the two
    wings of her story

still open. Still open, each moment bringing its own choice:
    here now the balsam chapel of blue swinging doors;

here now the light finger-touch of wind.

3.

How life stays us
with her brown shoe
and bird-like eye, and says
the world is perfect,
worn and slightly soiled, but still
a fair copy of all that you asked.

Why should I sit here trying to decide,
filling the page with more
abstractions
when the world I know is not abstract,
not a series of half-sighs. Nor is it weary.
The tasseled corn will wave again.
The great river (which I all day should
have seen) still bends to its task
of carrying and bearing forth. All this

grows more visible as I sort
from my window
the fields of rusted thistle, blackberry,
goldenrod and husk.

So why still unsure of my task
at this makeshift alter? I wanted to glean
whatever is left of my life, to locate
its green nerve in the river's sway -- in my *own*
sway. To sing in my *own* curves, but I am less
an extravaganza of stars and river
than what rises off the well's glinty surface.
Surely, all that was intended has been granted.

The sisters' blessing bears down
as I sit to write, to lift my pen …
How I wish I could say *"with no mistakes"*
and live like Keats
under the open, shut wings
of poetry's breath.

Dancing at Old Threshers'
- Diane Frank

Tangerine sunset floats low on the horizon.
The moon is orbiting around your hat.

I dance with you between rows
of early September corn,
your Amish beard a field of uncut hay.

I haven't memorized the map
of the constellations, but your eyes
are burning. The landscape of your muscles
ripples under your white muslin shirt.

You turn me two hands round
as the Great Bear rises in the sky
above your left shoulder.

There's a secret beneath my gingham apron,
a shower of falling stars
as we dance around the fire
kicking up the ground made hard
by late summer rain.

We orbit around the shapes
of our forefathers' stories --

a galaxy of seasons changing,
the stars a blur,
woodsmoke and wisdom whirling.

As we circle around each other,
the bear wakes up from his dreaming,
hears the tinny music
of hammered dulcimer floating south.

He pulls corn out of the husks
and you open your mouth.

The moon cracks like a pumpkin.

The sparks brush your skin
like a woman with turquoise beads,
tan muscular arms
and the secrets of your shoulders.

I am the goose shadow dreaming
of the day the universe began,
singing the music of the next creation.

Inseminating The Cows

- Diane Frank

With a wild and tender look in his eye
he told me that he is the one
who inseminates the cows.
At the only dairy in Iowa
where the cows have names like
Starfire Sari,
Utopia,
Aranyani,
and Eternal St. Faye,
they use semen from a bull with
87 daughters,
all good milk producers, he said.
You have to do it at the precise moment
when they are ready,
about 12 hours after they go into heat.
How do you know, I asked him.
He smiled. He said,
most of them go into heat together.
They play in rings
and even mount each other.
Utopia usually gets them started.
He said their personality totally changes.
Sita, for example,
normally a shy girl,

got so excited when she was in heat last year,
that she repeatedly mounted the bull.
He winked at me. He said,
I loved to watch them playing
but never saw them complete.
The bull had several children,
but they must have mated in the evening
or in a secret place.
Maybe he was a woman, I said,
in a previous life, and still shy.
But they sold the bull last autumn,
and now, he proudly told me,
they use semen from the best prize bull
in the country.
Ten dollars a straw.
Frozen to 323 degrees below zero
in liquid nitrogen
and ready to go.
After the cows go into heat,
you check the mucus.
When they're ready, it's long and stringy
and falls completely down to the ground.
First you put a glove on
all the way up to the shoulder,
and put your hand up her anus
to feel the uterus.
It feels a certain way when they're ready,
firm and toned,
and you know.
Then you take a straw in your other hand,
and gently put it up her vagina.
You have to find the cervix.
It's wet, hard, and cartilaginous
like a woman's. A human cervix

feels something like the bottom of your nose.
Well, a cow's is something like that, he said.
You have to find the opening,
which is very small
and sometimes difficult.
Then you insert the straw
in exactly the right place,
deposit the semen,
and you massage her uterus
for a while with your other hand
so it will take.
Then you know the act is complete
and you leave the cows dreaming
of strong bulls and loving afterplay.
As he tells me, his farmer's hands
are around me
and he massages my left foot
in slow circles
as we lie on my Japanese bed.
I wonder how many men
could describe a human woman's body
with such tenderness and accuracy.
I wonder if he would make
as good a father for human babies.
And he is wondering
about the shapes of everything
inside my white Victoria's Secret nightgown.

Planting Flowers in the Intuitive Garden
- Diane Frank

I didn't plan where to put the irises.
The bulbs went in like a snowfall,
and two seasons later
when squawking geese shadows
flew south across the moon,
poppy seeds scattered where they fell.

As the tangled roots of warmer weather
push their way to the surface of the field,
daffodils collide with tulips.
Blueberries twist their branches
around rose petals
like a dancer who has stretched so far
beyond her natural shape
that the form has to break.
I dance in the garden at night
with pink lace climbing my ankles
and my toes bruised like blueberries.

Every day I add another flower --
columbines surprising the lattices on the porch,
shasta daisies with double rows of petals
wild as ostrich feathers or snow,
nasturtiums with edible blossoms.

Summer comes in a flood, but the wind is still breathing
with dahlias curling their leaves toward unknown colors.

I want to make love in the intuitive garden,
with peonies bent to the ground
by thunderstorms.
I want to dance in a gallery of angels
surrounded by wildflowers
and a pasture of goats and sleep.
Every day I add another flower
like the petaled surprise of love.
Every day the magenta blood of wild berries
stains my fingers and my cheeks.

Requiem for a Pond
- Diane Frank

The prairie grasses are starting to grow back
in the vacant field under the arching
Japanese bridge
where the koi pond used to be.

The hot summer winds move across
patches of red clover,
goldenrod and hepatica
where beaver and muskrat
built bridges across
the tributaries of a stream.

Goodbye to evening walks
clapping my hands on the bridge,
tossing pieces of fresh-baked bread
to the carp and catfish.

Goodbye to elderberry blossoms
in humid summer heat,
cicadas in loud cacophony
rising and swelling
through moonlight streaming like ribbons
across the humid air.
Farewell to long-necked swans

who led their babies
across these shallow waters,
to the lone Canada goose
breathing her last gasp of air.

Farewell to weddings in the pagoda
by the water.

Farewell to the black water snake,
the bending arms of the weeping
willow, the lantern yellow
underbellies of box turtles.

Goodbye to the unh unh unh
of bullfrogs.

Goodbye to the green wings
of hummingbirds above sunflowers,
lilies, and black-eyed-susans,
to the blue whirring
of dragonflies skimming the water.

Goodbye to new lovers
walking over the arching bridge
for the first time together. Goodbye
to solitary dreamers longing for hands.
Goodbye to my reflection
in the water.

The night they drained the pond
students carried the fish
in bowls and buckets
to the closest river.
Now the wind is a paintbrush

over the memory of water.
Goodbye to constellations
reflected to an earth
that is sleeping.

Children play hide and seek
in the woods where
they're cutting down old growth trees
to build new houses.
Farewell to the memory
of tree frogs.

Candle boats scatter roses
below an early evening
swimming with fireflies.
Goodbye to the full moon
reflected on these waters.

Goodbye to the souls
of the trees.

Winter Prairie
- Jeffrey Hedquist

I tucked in this grassland
beside me, with iron, mulch and love.

Snow awakens winter visions
like cat dreams.

Wild bergamont seeds fresh from Autumn's shattering
wait in frosted thatch,
hoarding magenta ribbons for the celebration of warmth.

Prairie fingers dig deep to pull jewels from the clay.
Hawk glides slice the wind thick with spirit.

I never thought I could be your lover
But here I am
with tears streaming,
deep in frozen mush by the Walnut Creek.

You make a good soup.
Now, we can walk on the pond.

Bill Loves the Light
                              - Jeffrey Hedquist

(souvenirs from the temple ceremony)

For Bill Teeple

On this crackling December night
we are drawn from the snowy sky
into the white-walled gallery.
Follow his hand
taste the beauty of his pencil creations
and share his laughter -
souvenirs from the temple ceremony.

Inhale the spark,
pulled in
to tiny squares
and spaces.

Miniature tectonic plates of graphite
fold over each other.
Each pass, a feathered
layer of feeling.
Shadows play with edges

as he caresses the teeth of the landscape
with music heard only by paper.

The symphony arches
the white room swelling
with dark valleys
and hopeful mountains

Eyes to paper
wrist blurring
fire dancing, life breathing lines,
fingers pulling through the muscles,
heart pouring fabric
beneath a pencil point.

He cups the smoldering sky in his hand
tinder in his words
teasing flame from the dark.

Each addition breathes us
in, out, moths
ready to die in the light.

Bok Choi
- Jeffrey Hedquist

Twenty below, wind like a knife
I struggle through Iowa's January.
The hoop house door cracks
with an arthritic sigh.

Inside in the gray light
a silent grave of vegetation
Anyone home?

Off in the northeast corner
one cold frame hints at
green community within.

Oh!
Ancient tales of fierce warriors
pale in comparison to your courage
oh noble Bok Choi
proudly defiant, green, alive
pushing hopeful heads through crystalline
humus!

My outpourings frost the air.

The vegetables look up.

Yes, something we can do for you?

Humbly I lower the glazing
and continue crashing about in the winter garden.

Neglected Desire

- Christine Schrum

It starts with a flickering,

the spark-tipped tongue of a lighter
licking the wick of your decision
to live carefully.

Waxen plans collapse to the floor.
The elaborate candelabra
fashioned with pain-fearing fingers
trembles as it teeters off the table,
taking the drapes down with it.

Next thing you know,
the whole damn house is in flames.

The neighbors can see you.

You are naked and burning
and laughing,

rising from the slag like a redwing blackbird,
obsidian feathers iridescent in the light,
a warbling in your throat
like molten pebbles
in the windpipe of a river.

For Janna

- Christine Schrum

(in memorium)

If words could weave braids,
I'd write the golden rope
you tossed over a shoulder each day,
hopping down from your Dad's pickup truck
(the chariot that carried you
from horse pastures to first period in tenth grade).

Your wool skirt, brushed with the fine straw
of dog hair, made me sneeze every morning.
I sat beside you anyway, religiously
inhaling your honeysuckle scent like
field lilies, buttercups,
the yellow blossoms of wild marigolds.

Janna, if language were a loom
I'd thread memories together
until the soft shawl of your arm
draped across my shoulders one more time.

Couldn't look you in the eye
the night I stole beer from the corner store,
fearing your gentle disapproval
would turn the sky tornado green,

tumble me upside down
through oceans churning with corn and cows,
cheeks burning with prairie dust.

If you were here you'd say,

Forget about that. Write instead
about how we danced

at school during lunch break,
when Jen Howland practiced that song

Fur Elise

on the clunky piano
and the notes were so tinny
because the keys were old and stiff
but she plunkered through it again and again

and we danced

a kind of waltz,

more spinning than anything,
your palm in mine,
skin cool as morning dew,
the bale of your hair
flung loose like hay

and we danced

dizzily whirling and laughing
like thread on a spinning wheel,

spinning and

spinning.

The Seeker

- Christine Schrum

There's a cricket in my room tonight.
A moment ago, he appeared
on the soft green pillow
just inches from my face.
A black-eyed stare
the undulation of thread-thin antennae
and off he sprang.

Now I can hear
the rubber stamp of his body thumping
against hardwood floors and wall plaster,
tapping a morse code message
in invisible ink.

I want to take him outside,
let him join the throng
of black-faced fiddlers
rubbing their limbs together
under the full moon, hushing
the rush of steel and human desire
hurtling down Highway 34
a block north.

I want to cup his spry body

in my palms and feel the urgent jumping
of his legs as I descend the stairs
slip out onto the porch
and release him into darkness
and possibility.

Clifford Gibson

- Christine Schrum

Sometimes I still see the crescent moon of his toothless
	profile,
my mother's white hands slipping his dentures out at night,
long, silver strings of spit trailing like shooting stars.

I hear the heaving of a coal-miner's lungs,
the putter and sput of an engineer's cough
barreling through his chest like a sooty steam engine,
rumbling for miles into fir-trees, rocks,
the bull-headed heart of the Cambrian shield.

I feel Vaseline Intensive Care for bedsores, slippery
beneath my fingers as I massage the smooth, hairless skin
on legs that skied past silver foxes and sleeping birch,
skimming the pine-prickled lip-line of Lake Huron.

I remember tales of gunning down moose,
of gutting perch, of saving my mother from a bear.
Tales of pitching tarpaulin in starlight,
of watching my sister eat her first vanilla cone,
tales rasped over the burble of oxygen tubes and catheter-
drain.

I remember the crawdad grasp of my Grandfather's hand,

the tired man tolerating a bed with bars a few days longer
so his granddaughter could fly in from Iowa for one last
visit.

Most of all, I recall the extreme relief mixed with regret
each night, stepping out of the tepid cloud of antiseptic,
boiled beef and potatoes,
the rotten vegetable smell of the dying,
into the arctic chill of January, the sky spilling stars
and spitting snow squall in my face, stinging my eyes
as I walked past Grandpa's window and, squinting,
saw him hold out a blind hand
and wave goodbye.

The Non-Believer

- Christine Schrum

All my friends are pairing off
like zebras and sheep
two by two
linking lives nose to tail
trotting down the aisle
toward a white ship that will save them
when God gashes the floodgates apart
with a roar.

And here I am --
the lone jackass
stubbornly sloshing around
in the rapidly rising waters,
hooves soaked and split,
trying to find a
sturdy bale of hay.

Won't Need To Say A Word
                                              - Robin Lim

In 1978 I lost the honey bear.
It was sitting on the window sill,
sunlight trying to penetrate the thicker golden,
then it was gone.
I found her in the garden.
Baby was squeezing the viscous sweet
onto the backs of big zucchinis.
Lying on her belly
she was tasting green stripes.
Inside my chest is a snapshot
of the dirt stuck to her two year old face,
when she turned toward me that summer.

Tonight my daughter sleeps.
Blue parchment eyelids
fold over all she has seen,
and kiss her vision goodnight.
I inspect her arms, finding some purple.
Curled between her breasts
my granddaughter exhales,
then her breath stutters in again.
They smell unhappy.

This is my house enfolding them.

So I sip a hot cup of vinegar,
counting my strong feelings,
watching them hanker for blood.
So many scarlet demons
hunch down
in the mud trenches of my heart.

Once, when this girl
was still eating at my breasts,
I prayed for the red-headed mother
of the man she would marry.
I hoped that where ever she was,
she would love her son enough.
Enough to teach him tenderness,
manners, loyalty.
She taught him to love black cars and guns.

I forgot to give my daughter a filter.
I forgot to say, "Some people are just plain bad."

Sitting in the morning garden,
before they wake,
I make a witch's plan to feed my generations.
Borage flowers, like cobalt stars to guide them.
Kale, nourishing, curly and bitter green, like life.
Fat tomatoes, circled by purple
and yellow johnny jump-ups.
The new baby can watch the corn
reaching toward August.

Stoop Berries
- Robin Lim

Grandma Levon and Great Aunt Etha
are no longer able to harvest
the black raspberries.

On the 4th of July in Fairfield, Iowa,
it's well over 100 degrees out there by the fence.
The tangle and thorns call to the sisters
with finger staining promises
and memories of pies
cut and portioned out decades ago.
Pies that made now-dead husbands
lick their fingers
and bear up to the humidity.

This particular year Levon's grown granddaughter,
Rebecca, braves the berry patch.
She stoops to the lower brambles
where the big berries cluster.
Etha's cinnamon-colored cat
teaches her to bend even lower
to where the sweetest fruit hides.
Rebecca leans in farther, thorns catch her blouse.
Looking over her shoulder, she smiles
with purple mouth.

They see her through a pane
of glass and heat ripples
evaporating the day.

When the young woman turns back too quickly,
gets scratched and bleeds,
Levon and Etha touch hands.

Painting Carolyn's Bedroom in August

- Robin Lim

Last Easter she called, confused. "Can't keep food down.
Need help with a suppository. Can you come?"

I brought a small basket of hard-boiled eggs and one latex
glove.

Until today, I've never admitted to myself that I resented
being asked to insert that suppository. I was feeling selfish,
eating chocolate Easter rabbits with my children.

Carolyn had longed for a cherry red rag rug which caught her
eye in a little shop by the Des Moines River, in Bentonsport.
When the trees were bare in that part of Iowa, she would go
there to count eagles. That day she saw fourteen predators.

When the headaches began, we went out for the medicine of
pumpkin pie. She took hers without whipped cream -- she
was watching her weight. We blamed her illness on the
disappointment she felt when someone else bought her rug.
"Thou shall not covet thy neighbor's red rag rug." We
laughed and boiled more water for tea.

I'm painting the ceiling apricot, it was her favorite color. In
an apricot silk dress I saw her, before we were friends. She

was an almost beautiful blond woman. Her feet appeared pearl-like, and she floated above these small white camellia appendages, as if she did not want to burden them.

The walls are the color her son calls "rice cakes." When I opened the can and looked into the round white, I recalled how she turned her bottom toward me, toward the medicine she needed, twisting gracefully, keeping her blue eyes on my face.

I did the dishes. Dried my hands. Started a load of laundry and called the neurologist.

"I don't care if the MRI was normal." Knowing the doctor was home for Easter Sunday I continued recording, "Your idea that Carolyn's symptoms are psychological is half-baked. Dig deeper for Christ's sake, get a bigger shovel."

She would not sleep another full night in this room. We called an ambulance. She fought getting in, like a cat being forced into water.

In a corner her ashes wait in a box, to go to the river.

It's Fall again. Carolyn's son is walking out onto the bridge that joins Bentonsport to Vernon township. He throws his mother's remains over the edge. Down river a woman sees something white, the color of rice cakes, swirling, sailing by. She's been out in her yard, beating her rag rugs.

Overcast
- Robin Lim

When the stardust of lust
rolls over in their bellies
I have nothing to offer.

These tornado days of spring
are dark and hot, humid
as my memories of Indonesia,
but I am hobbled in Iowa dream-time.

Out in the garden plot,
below the dead leaves
lies a fecund bed for seeds.

Half these women left
their men,
then returned to be impregnated.

How do the upside-down
children feel about their origins?

Does God love all the unplanned,
unintended, accidental angels?

As their midwife

I have washed my hands
so many times that the bones
and knuckles must frighten the newborns.

I wish the sky would open,
would have the courage
to just haul off and hail.

Ode to Fruit Cake Baker
- Robin Lim

Late in July Edie picks yard pears
slices and dries them, shriveled moons on wire racks.
By August something signals her to begin saving
the rinds of oranges.
On September first she shops for pecans,
black mission figs, medjool dates from the Holy Land,
a bottle of strong foreign rum, cherries.

Across the street children assemble
for their first day of school.
She assembles the measuring spoons
her big blue crockery bowl comes down, she pauses
to consider how old the can of Baking Soda must now be.

The pans are wiped clean and lined
with waxed paper.
Black walnut ground-falls are gathered and cracked.
Flour should be fresh ground. A pinch
of salt brings out the orchid scent of vanilla bean, marries
it to the sugar.
She decides not to blanch the almonds
a little bitter is good.

He comes home from work

as the cakes emerge from the oven,
helps her pour the dark liquor over,
wraps each one in loosely woven cotton rag.

She posts one to a rural route in Oregon,
another to a P.O. box in Northern California.
The best one goes to the poet in Iowa. Hear the dark
eyes making notes on her cello.
How can the mailman know, on the day before Christmas,
what is so heavy? He drops a white
package on the snowy porch. The poet
will find it in a day, or a week, half buried
half frozen. In her hand she will feel the weight
of being the daughter Edie never had.

Grandma's '59 Oldsmobile

- Bill Graeser

had never been in the rain.
Garaged, showroom shiny,
driven only on sunny days
to the store, so that 30 years later

with just 17 thousand on the odometer
men throughout town would say;
"Lady you want to sell that car?"
Then hit from behind

the car totaled, and grandma
never again with the strength
to go anywhere, bedridden
in a home, except on a rare day

when with tiny steps clutching
the walker, up the long hall all the way
to the front door, as if to drive
that shiny world once more.

The Secret
- Bill Graeser

can not be told
even if bellowed like a foghorn
no one hears
but the muttering in their head.

Yet when we are ready
deliverance speaks,
then, knowing,
we want to shout it

still no one hears.

So we learn to know quietly
and here and there
as we go our peaceful way
someone sees our smile

and asks.

The Town Clock

- Carole Lee Connet

She was too poor to buy a clock,
so when the baby woke to nurse,
she'd roll over on hip bruises made by the oak floor
pressing through their thin army blanket mattress—waiting
for the chiming of the courthouse clock to break
darkness into segments short enough to promise light.

Through the window
she could make out one of the four faces
above the leafless limbs of trees, a friendly ghost
beyond the tracks that split the town in half,
a pair of arabesque hands falling in a never-ending circle—
apart, together.

Like clockwork the coal train woke her, shaking
the oak planks, the plaster, the narrow panes
so hard she was sure the house would crack and crumble.
It took the tolling of the bronze bell in the red granite tower
to comfort her back to sleep.

Sometimes other babies woke her. She caught them
as they fell out of the dark tunnel.
Halfway between wife and angel,
midwife, kneeling between sleeping deities

and the crashing, swarming world.
Often, the nightmare woke her. The frozen
tableau of gossiping neighbors,
sleeping dogs on the hot blacktop,
the untimely truck, the boy on a bike
in midair, throwing her baby to his father, running to catch

a six-year-old falling from the sky,
her brown hands reaching for noon or midnight,
the wind of his body grazing her breasts,
crumpling, no blood, his beautiful face looking up at her,
then

closing his eyes
as she kneels to hold him,
everyone frozen in a circle around the Pietà,
except the boy's mother,
running in a white bathrobe, not knowing.

The clock's hands stopped moving when she moved away,
each pair frozen in a pleading position.
What if she had run faster?
What if she could reverse time?
Or was she already too late?

When she moved back to town,
the silence woke her.
It woke the man with black fingernails
fleeing a ghost in the moon. He could fix anything broken,
almost anything. He climbed the fragile iron ladder

into midair, more than once. A miracle
for a woman afraid of falling.
He saved the town clock.

The bell tolled, the hands moved in pairs,
all the faces lit up.

High Flying Geese

- Ray Clines

To take the pulse of the prairie
Strip the soil from a stem of wild grass and listen:
Thousand-year cadence of silty silence –
deep, visceral, loamy.
A silence compressed by glaciers and ice-age eons
Woven deep enough
To beat beneath frozen rivers.

Plants root in this alluvial stillness
In the silent significance of decay
In the breakdown of shadow and ash
And come up spinning and clacking in the wind
Throwing their seeds at the sun
And high-flying geese.

Break it open, plow deep
Shovel up the Silence in rich dark clumps.
Clean off a rock and put it in your mouth -
Taste the freedom.

As he lay
- *Graham de Freitas*

As a baby he lay
quiet for once
on his back with his tiny hands clasped across his chest
in the middle of his parents' huge bed
as the cool breeze brought the sounds
of the neighborhood in the window,
thinking of who knows what.

As a boy he lay
under a favorite tree,
on his back with his hands clasped across his chest
thinking of clouds and baseball and miracles.

As a young man he lay
on his back with his hands clasped across his chest
with his head (just a little heavy) on the lap of a girl,
thinking of love and of clouds
and of her hair which fell from her head
like the branches of a weeping willow.
while inside her had just begun the miracle
that produced in just a few months --

a baby who lay
on his back with his tiny hands clasped across his chest

in his parents' huge bed
as the breeze brought sounds in the window,
thinking of who knows what.

As a father he and his son lay,
after the wrestling and the game of catch,
on their backs with their hands clasped across their chests
talking of clouds and baseball and ice cream.

As an old man he lay,
after he had died peacefully in the night,
on his back with his hands clasped across his chest
thinking, perhaps, or who knows what.

And his son climbed up
and lay beside him for a while,
on his back with his hands clasped across his chest,
thinking of loss and change,
until he took his tears outside to his favorite tree

and lay
on his back with his hands clasped across his chest
thinking of tears and clouds and trying not to think,
until his girl (who knew his favorite places)
appeared above him
with her hair falling like willow branches
and he managed to smile
and later to think of clouds and miracles
and who knows what.

Everyday Walk

- Graham de Freitas

the way the body goes
is down beside the pond
the gentle fountain
and the waterfall
up to the road and down again
under the trees by the school
turn left after the red brick house
and there's home

the way the mind goes
is high above the earth
in two giant strides
I'm home

the way the bliss goes
I am home already
and I never leave

Deja Vu

- Graham de Freitas

Bending,
as so often before,
to move the heavy bottle on the tile floor,
as so often before,
among the aeons of my deeds and misdeeds,
in this place where I sowed
the present in so many pasts
and am sowing now the seeds
of weariness tinged with awe,

lifting now,
as so often before,
cradling the big blue,
as always,
flashing on memories
of crack and splash and shards of glass,

and walking
as before,
back to the lights of the world
and the present order of my joys and cares.

Polishing the Quiet

- Susie Niedermeyer

I feel my roots reach deep into the Iowa soil
as I walk this afternoon, drinking in
the roadside slash of blowing grasses,
the muddy fields, grey skies. In my blood
I feel the sentient force of tiny seeds,
embryos flung out like light under the winter
houses of the zodiac. Don't you feel the dark,
wet kiss of the soil that surrounds them?

I watch three vultures float overhead, poised
on air and crying their darkness, their shrieks
bright with blood as they scissor down
to feed on a hunter's refuse,
wary and inscrutable, slate eyes blank
as the shadow side of an empty mirror.
Hopping along, already too bloated to rise
they flap at dark turkeys that erupt
in a burst of wingfire and vanish,
gabbling in the bush, all part of the crumpling
of words into a oneness bigger than the sky.

I hold small stones in my hand
in the shadows of late afternoon.
The sky melts pink on the dark tongue

of the pond and here, alone, I want to know
unseen things. Hear the violin
that closes its eyes and gives its lips
to a pale, melting fire, tender earth,
beading rain, ever polishing the quiet
in a slow tango, adoring the world.

Lake Keosauqua

- Susie Niedermeyer

A praying mantis hangs
on a branch over the water
as we float on our backs,
the drops on our eyelashes
refracting afternoon sunlight
into orbital moons
that reconfigure with every blink.
Our lidded eyes issue invitations
in the language of lovers,
pale legs frog kick
bringing us near
or shyly spurting us away.
We are held in the body
of the lake, its seminal liquid
transmitting every libidinal rift,
far from the bottom line,
tired bodies and the sticky
adherence of guilt. All we know
is the slow rush of the mind
and the variegated light dappling the skin
of the water under willows,
tempering the voltage that desiccates
carrion and cracks the soil.
And there on a floating twig

like a ripple of memory
is a moth with furred antennae,
and wings of chameleon flames
dotted with empty eyes
of white. Watching it preen
with thinnest jointed limbs,
I lose myself in dream and slap
of tide. But don't be fooled,
this incandescence lasts five days
at most, and needs only air
and a floating other
to transmute its fragile genes,
something we do better on land
and call by quite a different name.

Directionless
- Lucia Rich

I can't figure how to work it,
this field of unknowing,
blowing in wave after wave
of endless choice,
with no shore to rest upon.

I could be like a dandelion seed,

floating along
in a whimsy of wind --
or like a waterfall,
with no particular
destination
except down.

Everything sticks to me,

my body picks up lint
like adhesive tape.
If I fell in the snow,
I'd leave a dusty
angel print.

How can I choose which way to be?

no matter where I turn,
the wind blows hair in my face.
no matter how far I twist,
I can never see
past my right shoulder,
the light is never
bright enough
to make out the troops
of possibilities,
lining up behind me
in the mirror.

If only
I could keep twisting
in
towards the center,
then I'd know what if feels like,
to be
in the eye of the storm,
with no up
or down,
just clean space,
where it's clear,
and still,
like sky before dawn.

Out of Darker Grace
- Freddy Fonseca

"No one regards what is before his feet;
we all gaze at the stars."

- Quintus Ennius

When the universe withdraws
behind the dark, and
nothing else remains in space,
the stars across the sky
resume their ever-loving,
age-old wake.

Quietly, with unmatched care
since time one time
began its secret, outward dash,
they calmly gaze upon
the unborn realms of night
among the worlds.

Darkness must have been a cause
until this round, but
now that time has seen what was,
recalling what seemed
forgotten long ago, it's

like a darker dream.

Fully aware of the
mirage revolving around the
steady inner glow, a
deeper force unfolds despite
whatever gloom had
ever ruled before.

Remnants of an age lie strewn
across the sky,
but newborn lights are taking
full possession of the space
between what is to come
and darker grace.

Starry nights perhaps have
known it all along, for
deep inside themselves they've found
a way to manifest
and form from light and dark
the firmament.

Wisdom must have been their share
and warmth at heart,
and being of such service here
is maybe all they want
as time goes by on earth and brings the dawn.

After a Swim
- Freddy Fonseca

"There comes a time in the affairs of man when he must take the bull by the tail and face the situation."

- WC Fields

Here in the belly of the shark
It's really a bit too late
To worry much whether
I locked the door before
I left home this morning—
I'm most surely securely
Locked inside now, but . . .
If I ever come back to
Spook and check on things
With all the different parts
The shark divided me into
Before swallowing me
All up, I still have all my
Keys rattling in my swimsuit—
Now where did my hand go?

Thirteen Ways To Write Haiku -- A Poet's Dozen

- Ken Chawkin

I
Defined

3 lines, 2 spaces,
17 feet to walk thru;
then, the unending

II
Discovered

a poem unfolds
as words take their place in line
this one's a haiku

III
Transformed

Caterpillars spin
increments of commitment;
Butterflies fly free!

IV
Translated
(Inspired by a Gareth Jones–Roberts painting
"Egrets in Morning Light" — Australia)

on the edge of space
two egrets in morning light
woken from a dream

V
Galiano Island

West Coast Island Time
Nothing Moves, Nothing Changes;
Roosters Crow At Noon!

VI
Cliffhouse Deck at Dusk

Tiny bells call me
Arbutus blossoms falling
Sounding the Silence

VII
The Fall

sudden drop of leaves
a negligée to the floor
trees stand stark naked

VIII
Forest Flowers

tiny white flowers
a constellation of stars
so low yet so high

IX
Be Spring

Brown Branch Bursting Buds
Beneath Benevolent Beams
Boughs Bearing Beauty

X
I Wonder

Do trees have a say
When to drop anchors away
As ripe acorns fall?

XI
Winter Memo

On seeing snowflakes
written on a piece of bark
I copied this down

XII
Foggy Perception

a yellow raincoat
from out of a thick white fog
appears   to be seen

XIII
Concrete Impression

cement truck droppings
on the road   solidified
like elephant dung

Requiem For The Reservoir

- Karla Christensen

Where for twenty years students walked
a small path twisting among wildflowers
in grass thick and tall as windwaves
and sometimes catching the wild prairie ecstasy
have been propelled to dance the circular
movement and shine of grass in wind and sun,
now hardens rock, truck and tractor print on empty ground.

Let us say the names of the dead:
Big Bluestem, Black-eyed Susan, Yellow Puccoon,
Golden Trefoil, Brook Flower, Wild Ginger.

Where mothers and daughters gathered
lakeside to mold dolls of grass and mud,
decorated with stick and pine cone,
left for the sun to season, and where willow
lent crowns to weave flowers for our hair,

Let us name the dead: White Baneberry
Soloman's Seal, Hepatica, Trillium, Moonseed.

Where a flock of Canada Geese
balanced on thin ice under the sheep's-back sky
and the mud refused to dry in that turn

By the tall and thickly woven grasses
where we bathed our long interned winter feet
in the first mud of spring,

Let us name the dead,
Blue-false Indigo, Large-flowered
Prairie Beardtongue, Indian Grass.

Where the blue heron, knee-deep in water
and mud at the edge of the marshy cattails
stood so still we thought him one of the wooden
carvings a local artist makes, and thinking that,
walked until we stood eye to eye
before he sailed away.

Where once he fished for food
now lie rocks placed by dump trucks
run in tractor ruts over stem, weed and seed.

Let us repeat the names of the dead; Sweet Cicely
Indian Paintbrush, Blue Flag Iris, Bunchberry,
Columbine.

The Blue Fool
- Johan Svenson

I

There is no such thing as cities.
New York is just a thousand small towns
right next to each other.
Fairfield, Iowa is two.
God is what you get when you pack everybody
so close that they're in the same place
and sprinkle that place everywhere.
Funny then that God can seem so far
in shanty downtown high rises
and so close on the prairie.

II

We are surrounded by ten thousand people.
but this is no small town.
it is a nexus of far travelers,
a hub of worlds.
Here have come lovers and misfits,
saints and the insane.
Near where you now sit
twenty beautiful Africans

once celebrated life.
We've had singers and surfers
tossing discs
where years of sage laughter echoes.
There have been those
who've romped in the barroom
and those who've cried in the sun.
From the clear air of Tuva
and the ripe green of Hawaii
they've come to this little place
of no saltwater
but ten thousand shores.

III

Welcome back far wanderer.
Sit where you once did and remember.
Here we melt the scars of the journey,
and laugh at the redness of blisters.
The lay of the old road
spirals in the mist
of your steaming mug.
Children delight in songs
of your narrow escapes
and wide visions.
What sweet sorrow
that thoughts of unnumbered loves
flock in the silence
between your hearty stories
to rest in pools
at the foot
of tired eyes.

The Water Tower
- Matthew MacLeod

Perhaps longing for a birds-eye-view
of the endless golden prairie
she found herself in the town's water supply
one evening at sunset, 1000 miles from the sea

The silver rungs of the ladder had cooled
she climbed the sad excuse for a beanstalk
took a breathtaking view, and plunged
into the cool darkness of the town's precious tapwater

Overnight
all the small town men fell
head over heels in love
as they showered longer
drank bottomless pitchers of home-made lemonade
watered their lawns on the hour
loosened their wedding rings
and volunteered to wash stacks of dishes
spoons, forks, knives and pots and pans for their wives

Needless to say, the town's water supply soon diminished
the story splashed the front page of the local paper
people received fat tickets for past use of sprinklers
fountains dried up

swimming pools emptied
green lawns turned to a dull copper-bronze

All the small town men
walked the streets dehydrated
with whiplashed necks and wrinkled hands
searching for just a glimpse of her
or any body of water
until one day she drowned in mid-air.

Grasp
- Matthew MacLeod

the leaning grasp
the grasp, leaning further

split-second grip
into a side pocket

the croaking marsh frogs
the croaking marsh frogs left behind

late heatbug trill afternoon
abruptly leaving the woods

kicking stones back into the one gas station town
fixating on the sun-spotted coke machine

nudging the change button
eyeing the change slot

most days the pockets would be turned
inside-out Oliver Twist

curling the intent
pondering the pool hall

somewhere to talk the price of legs
something about blackberries

To Boot,
- Matthew MacLeod

I

That boot that I lost
at the edge of the pond
became an imagined catfish
and the talk of the town for years
before it was finally reeled-in
and revealed.

II

The other boot remained
on my foot for many years
until I, too, grew whiskers.

Prairie Madness
- Matthew MacLeod

After the old farmer lost his shirt in the spinning lights
at the Riverboat Casino on the curves of the Mississippi
after pulls of the *slot machines*, hits at the *blackjack table*,
turns of the *roulette wheel* and bluffs at *poker,*

He walked into the men's room,
unbuttoned his overalls,
and picked up a wrinkled copy
of the National Enquirer

When he had finished his business
The old farmer stood up,
took three steps back,
pulled out a pistol from his pocket,
aimed, and fired

A dealer rushed in suit
across the tiled floor.
"What the hell are you doing
Mister?" he shouted.

The old farmer lined up his gun,
took his next best shot at the porcelain
and replied,

"Son,
I was only shooting craps."

When I Fail To Remember Things

- Matthew MacLeod

When I fail to remember things
don't remind me
just take me out to an empty field
with the sparrows in the vanishing point and shoot me
full of country air

When I fail to see
don't throw your gaze down upon our silhouettes
just buy me a pair of inexpensive sunglasses
from the corner drugstore
the kind with tinted sides that Ray Charles
and outfield baseball players wear

When I fail to hear
don't speak in refrain
just turn up the radio as loud as you can stand it
in the middle of the night, at the break of day, anytime at all
yell at the top of your lungs as you say goodnight
then listen to the sparrows in the trees

When I fail to smell
leave the trash inside
bathe infrequently
pass wind often

let the leaning tower of dishes accumulate

When I fail to taste
we will dine upon whatever pleases you
breakfast, lunch, supper and tea
I'll eat sardines and alewives at the table's end while you
have caviar in saffron
with the money we'll save I'll buy you a famous painting,
a pearl necklace, a fig tree to put in the yard
and the world's loudest radio

When I fail to feel your touch
don't lose hold of yourself
take me in the cup of your beautiful hands
scatter me towards the sparrows in the trees
throw your pearl necklace to the stars
and invite over our closest friends to break all of the dishes.

The Poets

Tom LeMay was born on a sultry summer night in 1949 in New Jersey, the third son of Ernest and Joan LeMay who went on to have a total of 7 children. Since then Tom's been around the block a few times and currently resides in Fairfield, Iowa where he maintains a low profile.

Glenn Watt, as well as a poet, is a husband, father, Rolfer and fine wood-worker in Fairfield, IA. As this is being recorded, it is mid-spring, and he is drowning in warblers.

Steve Benson was educated at the University of Northern Iowa where he studied poetry with James Hearst. His chapbook "A Light In The Kitchen" was the winner of the 2001 Blue Light Poetry Prize. His poems have been published in Drumvoices Revue, The Mid-America Poetry Review, Wisconsin Review, Plainsongs, Comstock Review, A Different Drummer, Lyrical Iowa, Apalachee Quarterly, The MacGuffin and The North American Review. He teaches art in Mt. Vernon, Iowa where he lives with his wife, Darla and their two children, Chloe and Logan. Another son, Reid, lives in Boston.

Connie Larson Miller has been writing poetry for ten years. Her poems have been published in Lyrical Iowa, Eclipsed Moon Coins, The Alternative Scares Me and Iowa Heritage. She teaches visual arts and poetry for VSA Arts Iowa. She has studied at Indian Hills Community College and the Iowa Writer's Workshop. She currently lives in Ottumwa, Iowa.

Nynke Doetjes received her graduate degree in creative writing from San Francisco State University. Her work has been published in various literary magazines, among them 'Gulf Coast Review' and 'The Anthology of New England Writers'. Her Story 'The Kiss' was nominated for a Pushcart Prize in '96. She currently teaches creative writing and literature at Maharishi University of Management in Fairfield, IA, and is a member of the board of the New England Writers' Association.

Elisa Fritsch graduated from MUM with a degree in Literature that included minors in Art and Writing. She enjoys nature and likes to reassure herself of her own place in it. Elisa started writing poetry one year ago and has been relieved to find it such a broad field. Much of what she never termed poetry before has since fallen into that category. Poems like to fall out of her pens and do so whenever she finds time to set one to paper.

Tim Britton was born into a family central to the Philadelphia folk music revival. He has since become an acclaimed player and maker of the Irish uillean pipes and sometimes wordsmith. For the last twenty years he has returned from his touring to Fairfield, Iowa, where he lives with his wife Katie and daughter Mirabai.

Virginia McGuire has lived in Washington State, Hawaii, California and New Jersey since leaving Iowa in 1997. She is currently living in Philadelphia, where she is a librarian at Haverford College. One of her poems recently appeared in an anthology from CALYX Books, and another is forthcoming in an anthology from Pig Iron Press. She is at work on a novel.

Susan Klauber was born in Sudbury, Ontario in 1945, and has traveled and lived in many places around the world. Since 1983, she and her husband have made their home in Fairfield, Iowa, with frequent ventures to India. Susan is a physical education graduate of the University of Toronto, and has worked as a teacher, businesswoman and personal trainer. Her poetry and prose have been published in various journals and anthologies, including *The Mac-Guffin and Poetry Motel.* Her first book, *Face-off at Center Ice,* was published by Blue Light Press in 1997. She is currently working on a poetry manuscript, and a poetry/prose book about traveling in India.

Rustin Larson was born in Des Moines, Iowa. He was educated in Iowa and later earned an M.F.A from Vermont College of Norwich University. He is currently serving as a Poet-in-residence through the Iowa Arts Council. His poetry has appeared in numerous publications including: The New Yorker, America, Poetry East, Cimarron Review and Boundary 2. *Loving the Good Driver*, published by Mellen Poetry Press in 1996, is his first book. He lives in southeast Iowa with his wife, Caroline and their three daughters: Katharine, Sarah and Julia.

Michelle Demers holds an M.A. in Professional Writing Maharishi International University and an M.F.A. in Poetry from Vermont College. She has published poems in *The Urbanite, Collecting Moon Coins,* and many other publications. She currently teaches poetry and business writing at the Community College of Vermont in Burlington, Vermont.

Meg Hill Fitz-Randolph is a poet and teacher. Her work has appeared in a number of literary journals around the country including the Antioch Review. She teaches composition and writing courses at Maharishi University of Management. She recently spent a month at Ragdale, a working retreat for artists and writers, where several of her most recent poems were written. She lives in Fairfield, Iowa with her husband Tim and daughter Emily.

Diane Frank is an award winning poet, editor and teacher. She has mentored hundreds of writers at San Fransisco State University, City College of San Fransisco, the University of Vermont, and the Professional Writing Program at MIU in Iowa. She has written and published four books of poetry. *Blackberries in the Dream House,* her first novel, has been nominated for the Pulitzer Prize.

Jeffrey Hedquist is a poet, singer/song-writer, standup comic, MC, organic farmer, voice actor, seminar leader and radio producer who sometimes writes poetry in Fairfield, Iowa.

Christine Schrum is from Northern Ontario, Canada, where her childhood summers were happily spent ranging through under-brush, seeking out moose, and dodging black bears. She has since relocated to Iowa, whose lightning storms, seas of fireflies, and hot August nights have staked claim in her heart. She holds an M.A. in writing, a B.A. in literature and has published extensively in regional journals and anthologies. She currently covers rent by freelance writing.

Robin Lim is a mid-wife and poet. She is the author of *Stretch Marks* available from HALF ANGEL PRESS. In 2000 she won $500 from the National Federation of State Poetry Societies Contest, where Naiomi Shihab Nye was the judge, for her poem "Won't Need to Say a Word".

Bill Graeser is a poet and singer/songwriter. He performed through-out his native Long Island where he taught the Transcendental Meditation technique full-time for 16 years. Presently, Bill works as carpenter at Maharishi University of Management, Fairfield, Iowa, where he continues to write and perform.

Carole Lee Connet is a free-lance writer, editor, teacher, counselor, and perma-culturist. In 1996 she graduated with an MA in Professional Writing from MUM. Her poems have been published in Amelia, Lyrical Iowa, 100 Words, NYC Big Apple, and NFSPS Prize Poems. Her first book of poems, *Searching for Entrance* was published by Half-Angel Press. Carole lives in Fairfield, Iowa with husband John Connet, who repaired the town clock and rescued the organ in Barhydt Chapel. She has three sons: Jared, Seth and Noah.

Ray Clines teaches writing at Jacksonville University in Florida. He is a former Fulbright Lecturer to Thailand and author of several writing texts. He is currently on the Advisory Council for The National Writing Project in Florida. His poems have appeared in over thirty publications.

Graham de Freitas teaches Maharishi Vedic Science at Maharishi University of Management in Fairfield. He has been writing poems for himself and for friends for many years. Recently he has been writing mainly about experiences of growth of consciousness. His poems have been published in four editions of "Lyrical Iowa." In 2003 he will publish a collection inspired by his Ph.D. research called "These Flames that I Speak - Experiences reading Vedic Literature".

Susie Niedermeyer is a professional classical pianist. Her writing has been published in The MacGuffin, Lyrical Iowa, and The Sierran Magazine. She won 2nd place in a 2002 contest sponsored by the National Federation of State Poetry Societies. Susie lives in rural Fairfield, Iowa with her husband Thomas.

Lucia Rich lives somewhere in the realm of theatre, just beyond the edge of dance with a back-ground in improvisational dance, mask and mime. She has studied and performed both nationally and internationally, including performances in Edinburgh, Scotland as part of their renowned Summer Fringe Festival. She received her BFA in theatre from Maharishi University of Management. She is currently living in London where she is completing a MFA in Physical Theatre from Naropa University.

Freddy Fonseca has absorbed the histories and cultures of Greece, France, England, Germany, Spain, the Netherlands, Italy, and the United States through his travels and read extensively in five languages, including well over 10,000 poems. He has performed his poems often in concert with the accompaniment of musicians and dancers. He currently lives in Iowa.

Ken Chawkin, an award winning poet, draws his inspiration from nature and feels that the creative process is a collaboration between the two. He holds a BA in English and an MA in Education. He has taught TM, has been a Sales Rep, an Ayurveda Health Technician, a Park Caretaker, a Reading and Writing Facilitator, a Publicist and is a father of two beautiful children. But he is just a poet at heart.

Karla Christensen is a poet, educational writer, writing coach, editor, aromatherapist, group facilitator, meditation and writing teacher. She has published poems in literary journals and anthologies, four poetry chapbooks and several aromatherapy books. Karla lives with her four teenagers in Fairfield, Iowa.

Johan Svenson is a traveler, reknowned Physics Teacher, Poet and Harmonica virtuoso. He once worked on a fishing boat but has since come back to land. He has also been known to hackey-sack for hours on end and play the *Blue Fool*. He is currently at work on his first novel.

Ila Zeeb is currently completing a BA in Maharishi's Vedic Science at Maharishi University of Management in Fairfield, Iowa. She was born in Germany and has worked as a Maharishi Ayur Veda Technician in Germany and the Netherlands.

Matthew MacLeod was born in a boat-house on Georgian Bay in northern Ontario. He is a poet, singer-songwriter, kindergarten teacher and sometimes road hockey player. He first studied poetry with Erin Mouré at Concordia University in Montreal, Quebec. Matthew has published poems in Scrivener and Writing/Ecrits. His first chapbook of poems entitled "Nights At The Round Table" is available from Arboreal Press. He does not believe in crop dusting but he does believe in Peter Pan.